THE LOST LIFE

SURYA SAXENA/ AARCHI ADVANI SAINI

The first poetry anthology of Penaaki is currently being written. There isn't a definite subject for the anthology because, in my opinion, everybody can have thousands of thoughts at once. We appreciate you sharing your wise advice with us. Your words inspire us to develop further or to support your development. I'm hoping we can collaborate soon. The experience of working with you all has been very wonderful. I wish you everyone a prosperous future.

Regards

Penaaki

Contents

Contents

A Book by

Penaaki

Aarchi Advani Saini

Aarchi is a 20-year-old Indian girl with big dreams. If you ever meet her, you can observe it by seeing the spark in her eyes.

Her Journey from an ordinary girl to a young Author.

She was born on 25th March 2002. She is the second daughter of Sanjeev Advani Saini and Mamta Saini who taught her how to cherish one's dreams.

Right from a young age, Aarchi dreamed of an artistic career. But what exactly it was? She had no idea about it.

Things do change with time. Your past questions get their answers in the present. Guess what? The same happened with her too. During the last years of schooling, she finally realized what she wants to become; A writer.

From then on, she pursued her talent in writing as a hobby as she did not want her parents to worry about her studies. Sweet girl, right?

In 2020, everything stopped. Not for her, but for everyone. Covid-19 took people's lives, jobs as well as health. Fortunately, our writer got a chance to open her wings during the lockdown. She did not miss the opportunity to enhance her skills.

How? She worked as a creative writing intern and wrote in Your Quote where she explored her true talent in this field. Now, the outcome of her hard work is in front of you!

Publications

It was on July 15 of the year 2021 that Aarchi first published her book: " The Loads of poetry part-1 and part-2" with Thepencilapp. From then on, she has published multiple books like

Anjaan Ajnaabi (A Hindi prose) - English translation available

• Faith is All

• Life- A Beautiful Lie

• Confession

• The journey of Love

• It's all about destiny

• The street of paris

- Dark dead

- Papa (Hindi prose cum poetic)

- The cabalistic child

- The way to love

- The Loads of Poetry (Part 3)

- The way to love

- Error

- New self

- Lifeless life

- The quiet spirit

- Half dead

- Khwaab (Hindi prose)

- Stuck

Etc.

Her books Confession and The Loads of Poetry recieved the attention of a wider audience and became her best selling books.

To enjoy her write-ups, you can buy them online on various platforms like Flipkart and Amazon. (Ebooks are also available).

She has competed in numerous national and international events, placing second in the RIC (READ INDIA CELEBRATION). Additionally, she enjoys branching out and has a youtube channel where she expresses her love of poetry and short stories.

This is just a tip of an iceberg. Aarchi's story does not end here. She is putting efforts in writing books that one day become the Best-Selling books by winning everyone's heart. She has written 30 books till now. And the journey is still on.

1. Innocent Love

Years ago,
When we were tiny tots
Having fun just terribly lots
And laughter never had full stops
I remember a friend of mine,
We used to sit together, play and dine
People considered it all as an unusual sign
We played together, hugged each other so tight
Apart from all the fun, we had horrifying ego and fight
But at the end, we didn't feel to go away from each other's sight
In the weddings and occasions, we walked hand in hand
Everywhere, taking each other, together we used to stand
Looking at each other and we felt so happy and royal and grand
All these innocence flew away within us, with the passage of time
Looking at each other, we get embarrassed like committing a crime
We get offended when people remember the same thing, talking in mime
Our foolish acts are now taken so seriously by everyone around us
We are like the favorite gossip for them, anything regarding we to discuss

making fun of it, exaggerating it and repeating it at homes, trains and bus.

2. I'm now

I have never felt this before
I was not the same as I am now
baby, you have entered my core
Seeing you, my heart roar's Wow
Tiny bells ringing in my heart,
Telling me that you're the one I looked for
And I should never leave you apart
because, in the wild ocean of heart, you're my shore
It took me a lot of time to realize I have fallen for you
And now, I have lost all my senses, you're the only one I need
How to offer you my feelings, I had just no idea, no damn clue
So, I thought of penning down this, and I hope that you just
read
I have tied the knot of love with you in my dream,
Just hope to see you at my side
in the tunnel of darkness and sorrows, I found you as my gleam
Now, I just want to make you my bride.

3. Daughter's life

Till today, I was a flower blooming in your garden
And now, you are plucking me out of it, just dis hearten
Why did God create such a dilemma, to leave you behind
leaving the house where I was brought up, with new relations to
bind
I was your darling, a part of your soul, Will you be able to live
without me ?
Who will now bother you, fight with you or would prepare you
food & tea
Dad, why is a daughter's life so difficult ?
Why am I suppose to leave my hopes;
And still continue to walk above !

4. Loneliness

A bunch of herds
When searched on social media
When in doubt of something
Every definition available in encyclopedia
But, when I wish someone to
Be with me, I am left with empty hand
No-one to to understand or feel my
Emotions and I tend to build castles in sand
Loneliness thus became my friend
At least it stays with me till the end
Unlike others who at times just pretend.

5. Forever

A bond of Forever
When all of a sudden,
Someone matters the most
When someone's absence
haunts you like a ghost
When saying nothing means
everything, you don't need words to explain
And you start to enjoy the days,
you find their feel when it starts to snow or rain
When, being there with them till the end,
visualizing them with you even when your hairs turn grey
When you dedicate your success and happiness to their
faith, and when you heal sadness because of their pray
My friend, that's the essence of true love
that hits you once and remains forever
To find the one who'll tolerate you and never
leave you, because they are your precious treasure.

Surya Saxena

Surya, is a 23-year old Indian boy with sparkle dreams. If you ever meet him, you can observe it by seeing the spark in his eyes. His journey from an ordinary boy to a young author; He was born on 13th February 1999. Right from a young age, Surya dreamed of an artistic career. But what exactly it was? He had no idea about it.

And he want to become financially independent, from a very young age, he start working and try to built himself. Things do change with time. Your past questions gets their answers in the present. Guess what? The same happened with him too. During the last year, he finally realized his true potential and dedication towards writing. From then on, he pursued his talent in writing as a hobby as he did not want to loose his job or financial independence. In the year 2020, when everything stopped, but his dreams took his path to do something for him or to make his family proud.

Books that is published till now is - " Mere Lekh" and "Let's Fall In Love".

6. What if I die?

What if I die,
Will there be anyone waiting for me.
Will there be anyone who will remember me for the things i have
done for them,
Will there be sadness in between my people.
Will they come to my grave and offer me flowers and ask for
peace.
Will I be at peace?
Will everything will be resolve one day.
What if I die
And there will be no one who wants me to comeback,
At a get together they talk about me,
Will they tell my stories to eachother,
Will they take care of the things that i left behind.
Will there be anyone who will miss me.
What if I die,
Will you ever thing what kills me Am too gonna be alone in this
too.
What if I die Will you miss me;
Will they understand my story
Will they ask about the things what I wanted to do.

Will they celebrate my death
Will they become sad on my birthdays
Will they know how much I loved them
Will they understand my pain
Will they come and visit me again Will anything gonna change
for anyone
Or they will just move on with it
What if I die today
Will anyone ask about me
But that all doesn't matter now Cause i can't answer them I am
far far away.
If I die
I don't want anyone to cry Just write a letter and tell her who
am I Just say good bye And celebrate the life...
Good bye...

7. I Am Far Far Away

I am far far away
From the place at i use to be
There was a dream that i want to live
I want to live it with you
With you i want to go so long
So long its been you haven't said "hi" to me
To me that's all was a dream
A dream that you miss me
You miss me? Then tell that to me
But i can't hear you
Because am far far away
I am far far away from you.

8. The One I Love

Hey

Have you ever tasted the stars

Do you even know how beautiful they are

The whole universe is filled with them

If you looked at them, they are not too far

But then I saw your smile

The tears in your eyes

The beating of your heart which I found closest to mine

But you said please never cross the line

Yes I have tasted the stars and I know how beautiful they are

As long as you are

The one I love

The one I love

9. Love is a Drug

Love is a drug
Love is like a drug
You never know if you'll get addicted
It's a killer drug
If you overdose you're dead It's a healing drug
It takes the pain away
You never know when you'll get addicted to love
Until you meet that one person
That one person that makes time stand still
That one person who you can never get off your mind
That one person who you never want to give up on
Love is like a drug
You never know if you'll get addicted
It's a harmful drug
It causes pain It is a bitter drug
It leaves a sour taste in your soul
Watch out for love
Be careful who you give your love to
Because everyone is not worthy
Love is a drug
And once you fall and that's all.

10. I Can Feel Nothing

This empty feeling
I can feel the cool breeze,
I can see the birds
I can tell you stories
I can See the moon Shining
All the stars that are riding
The sound of the birds
The noise of the city
The hustel of the day
The vibes of the night
The Light of early morning
Everything around me is happy
Everything feels Complete

But it's inside me
I can feel nothing
I lost the sense
I lost the smile
I lost everything i have
The day I lost you
I can feel nothing
I can feel nothing.

Palak Chauhan

Palak was born on 21 February 2002 in Dhampur, Bijnor , Uttar Pradesh

She is daughter of Late Mr Devraj Singh and Mrs Kamlesh (Primary School Teacher) Writing poems which are emotionally depicted is her way of expressing emotions which are left unsaid or untold.

11. I'm yours

I am alone with the love of yours
You are my madness, you are cure
Friends are Treasures, I was wrong
These are like the winter's fogg
Everyone is fake, like letters on the lake
I brokened up to end and the fun they make
Day by day I update my heart
But without you it's coming error
Between us everything is over
Still my heart loose a hope never
You have forgotten me
But I am yours forever and ever.

12. Hey Moon Princess!

Hey Moon Princess!
I believe you there
Looking in to my prayers
No I don't want those twinkling stars
No I won't wonder how beautiful those galaxies are
That mesmerizing space is Just a Zero for me
The peace of my eyes is a person,
Who had reached your kingdom by mistake,
Yes your kingdom,
The kingdom of stars.
Ask your moonlight to find him
I'm waiting for his home coming.

Himanshi Soni

She is Himanshi . She has been writing for 2 years. She is a
student by profession. She comes from Haryana. She likes to write
love poems. A few of her poems has been published.

13. Love

1. How can we pick each other clearly?
Fate is tangled up in the corner
Love dosen't need any logic to think
Only the right pace
At the door of the heart ...knock knock
I want to make my own
Say good night for the rest of my life
I just want to smile, laugh and look at you
To be by your side
I want to be with you for the rest of my life...
2. In this place you're not here to wake me,
I've stopped moving, I'm waiting for you
I need your love, take me away
I need you now, please hold me tight
I'm crying alone, over the memories I've lost
I need your love, in your embrace
You're the only one who can wake me up
When this long night passes, I'll be lost again
I'll wait forever, In this place
I'll wait, always next to you
I want to hold your hand someday
I want to walk with you.

14. Smile

3. I smile today too, for no reason
Today passes too
The me that's filled with the sense of futility
The wounds you can't see
The days trapped in dark dreams
You who took me out, you light me
Maybe i need you, I need you
I wanna be yours
You who were in my dreams for a long time
In your eyes. Even though I'm not the person you see
Maybe i love you, I love you
Precious you and our memories, I remember them
The tears you can't see
You wake me up again
4. Those silly words, either intentionally or not
How can they be sweet when I say them
Turns out there is a few steps between us.
And we look back again and again
What a beautiful encounter
I become a better me because of you.
I want you to hear all of my mind
Whisper everything in your ear

I am no longer afraid of being
side by side with you in the noisy crowd.
You make my love so simple and obvious
The rushing time retreats, let happiness come to you
My heart wants you to hear.

Angad Kuaano

Angad Kuaano aka Kuaano Gorakhpuri

Software Engineer currently working for TCS. Writing from early age of 12. Currently based in Mumbai.

Active Languages : Hindi, Urdu, Punjabi, Bhojpuri, English, Saraiki.

Winner of National Level Literary Event "Slogan Writing" Organized by MRSPTU Bathinda.

Winner of National Conference 2022 organized by BCIPS.

15. Life

Life is sometimes harsh too much why …
Never I thought that I would cry…
But this is going So tough now God …
No one is here to heal or hold …
Why this is God, Why this God…
If I'm bad how you are not …
Love is so cheap frendship is trash …
Nowdays loyalty is on the cash …
While writing these I'm crying a lot …
Where are we going Give it a thought …
Why this is God Why this is God
If I'm bad how you are not…
You can forgive and give us a chance …
But Karma hits us and we just dance …
We are a bot here you wrote the code …
Why I'm apart from each of my node …
Why this is God Why this is God …
If I'm bad How you are not …
Why this is God Why this is God …
If I am bad how you are not …

16. Love or Attraction

It was love or attraction
I don't know what to say
I was young and childish
So I don't know the way
I made my own topology to you
I know I owe an apology to you
I haven't said yet
But there's a guilt in my head
I should say sorry personally in this case
But I know you don't wanna see my face
So I'm requesting pardon through poetry instead
Please forgive me for whatever I did
Please forgive me for whatever I did.

Hugh Conan Doyle

Hello. I'm Conan (preferred name) from the lovely city of Chennai. Not the most common Indian name but definitely one at heart and a true patriot. An aspiring comic who delves into intricacies of life to uncover its funny side. An HR by profession and an artist by passion, I spend a lot of my time thinking about my future if there would be any. I'm a good listener which probably why you'd see me on occasional long telephonic conversations instead of the short frequent bursts. My friends call

me a people person and I'd like to believe I am one.

17. Complicated - 1

There are times when I wonder, why me? Why was I chosen to be sported with a name

as complicated as "Hugh Conan Doyle"? I remember asking my father, "Couldn't you

have thought of something less complicated? Like an Antony or a Michael?"

Yes, I mean it. My name is Hugh Conan Doyle, 36 years old, married to my

organization10 years ago. My name is not the most common in India, so I do not expect

everyone to pronounce my name accurately. Expecting someone to pronounce my

name accurately is like expecting RCB to win an IPL tournament!

One of the biggest challenges of having a name like mine is that I get compared to a lot

of people. For example, I get compared to Sir Arthur Conan Doyle, the creator of

Sherlock Holmes. See, that is not fair. He had two wives, I had five backlogs in college.

He studied medicine; I consumed those medicines. He was a great writer, I was also a great writer; wrote several emails saying, "We will get back to you". Yes, I am from the

Human Resources Department.

One other person that I get compared with is Hugh Jackman. Why? Because both of us

bear the same first name, "Hugh". Now, that is not fair either. You are comparing a star,

a legend, and an icon to someone like Hugh Jackman? Unfair, right? I am a humble man,

after all.

Besides getting married, my name also contributed to a significant portion of my

otherwise depressing life. About 10-15 years back, when smartphones were not

available, that was the time Sachin Tendulkar and petrol were still fighting over who

would reach 100 first, I tried to book a cab. We did not have app-based rideshares then,

so I ended up calling a call taxi agent. Here's how the conversation went.

Agent: "Sir, your name please."

Hugh: "Hugh"

Agent: "Who?"

Hugh: "Hugh"

Agent: "Who?"

Hugh: "It's Hugh, damn it!"

A moment later I received a text message,

Booking ID: 43456

SURYA SAXENA/ AARCHI ADVANI SAINI

Booking ID: 43456

18. Complicated - 2

Name of passenger: Hugh damn it

Since then, my name in their company's records has been recorded as Hugh damn it.

It was not just in the outside world that my encounter with embarrassment was

apparent but also within office premises. One day, I was working inside a conference

room in the office (yes, we were physically present in the office and that indeed was a

different reality) when an employee suddenly barged inside the conference room and

yelled, "Who is Hug Canon here?"

Life can be hard on you sometimes and the pain can be felt the most when it starts with

stabbing your name with a plethora of mispronunciations. So, if there's one lesson I

have learned, if or when I become a father, I have decided to give him a less

"complicated" name. I have thought of "Mahershalalhashbaz". Any thoughts or ideas for

a better name? Because after all, what's in a name?

Mizna

It's me, Mizna! I'm a student exploring oceanography and one who lives with the wonder of nature. I have a passion for journaling. and I am a girl who just loves to write, travel and explore new places. I also study journalism and social media.

I love hearing from my readers and am always up for new ideas, so if you have any suggestions or requests, don't be shy—let me know in the comments below!

19. It's just another season

Do you know what's hard ?
The loneliness . The pain .
You never thought this was going to fall apart .
You didn't realize that there was a feeble stitch holding
everything together .
You never knew , but the one that got away It's you breaking
now .
It's you struggling to fill the void .
It's you gasping for breathe every night . did .
It's just you screaming for help ... to be saved from all this .
" Trust the process " this one angel said . Yes , you'll eventually
heal .
You'll carry a scar from this battle wherever you go .
You'll cry till you can't no more , but one fine day , you will get
up and decide that the storm has passed .
You'll find someone who will stroke your hair , whisper words of
truth , words of love and wake up next to you everyday .
This life isn't easy .
Everyone breaks at one point .
Remember , this is just another season . The best is yet to come.

20. It's a girl !

Shouts of joy , never heard
Whispers arouse and swirl
Through the village , like a bird
The infant's cry
Softened by mother's touch
Father's eyes dry
For he perceived too much
Marriage , dowry
Waiting a haste
The girl if let free
Will never return chaste.
The damsel's beauty
Will woo the ' charmings ' Protecting her , their duty
Deflecting the departing
In - laws ' facades quite dull
" I wanted you to have a son ,
To take the family line full Not a maiden to leave it and be
done.

Aliyu Nuhu

Aliyu Nuhu is a graduate of Botany, a agricultural surveyor and a multipotentialite Entrepreneur. His hobby is arts and traveling.

21. Arise a blissful individualistic

..."I Hear world Singing' presents a picture of countries that the worldwide residents might want to accept is valid a picture of glgad and solid individualists participated in useful and blissful work.

Technician, craftsman, bricklayer, boatman, deckhand, shoemaker, hatter, wood-shaper, plowboy-from city to country, from ocean to land, the 'changed tunes' mirror a certifiable euphoria in the day's imaginative work that makes up the pith of the Worldwide dream or legend. . . .

world singing arises as a blissful, individualistic, gladly procreative, and powerfully comradely world."

22. A Community once filled with regards.

I see, in lowlife,

The mother abused by her youngsters,

Passing on, disregarded, thin, frantic;

I see, in lowlife

The spouse abused by her better half

I see, in lowlife

The deceptive enticer of young ladies;

I see, in lowlife

How the legislator,

Use a majority rule government as weapon

To abuse the feeble

I mark, in lowlife

The ranklings of envy and lonely love,

Endeavored to be stowed away,

I see these

Sights on the earth"

Every one of these-All the unpleasantness and anguish

Endlessly,

I sitting, watch out upon,

It's obvious, I hear, and am quiet.

Where it counts in a called Arewa that was once loaded up with affection and regard.

· 51 ·

Anamika Sharma

She is Anamika Sharma. Anamika has been writing poems for more than 3 years and has been a content writer from the last 5 months.
She is one of the Top writers on Medium. She is a girl with big

dreams who believes that our actions can make this world a better

place to live in.

23. Shadows that Haunt

Daunting memory of the past,
Of same genre, different cast,
This movie, oh my god so vast!
Donnow which scene will be last.
Don't we all feel this way some way?
Journey of ups and downs they say
Just keep going is only what they weigh,
But sometimes, healing is what we pray.
I too have been hurt by someone close,
Someone, whom I love and trusted the most,
My most vulnerable days, feelings he knows,
Yet seeing him hurt me, made me all froze.
It hurts knowing, i wasn't a priority to his heart,
So close, yet his actions made me feel apart,
Sudden drift, change - new journeys impart,
After all, it was a post era in me about to start.
Staying with me is all I wanted from him,
A partner like him, is a blessing, truly a dream.
In his love, even a deadly ocean i can swim,
For me, life and love, of him is a synonym.
He decided to walk away for his own goal,
Without informing me, it took a major toll,

In our beautiful fabric of love, got a hole,
I'm hurt but he walked out taking my soul.
Today, the time may have started to race,
Our relationship is going with its own pace,
But in the closeness are moments of space,
It takes time to heal when damage is in base.

24. Remembering You

Standing here in the heat,
the warmth, tastes burning hot
on the face, making me sweat. But,
the noisy waves crashes the shore.
Smell of the sand makes me lost,
in a world where all's good and nice.
But, the scorching heat brings me back,
though, the coral protects me under
it's branch like an umbrella
on a rainy day.
"You protect me even today?"
I say, looking up, as you stroke
a red blossom down my cheek. Watery eyes,
when about to burst, a splash hits me;
Briny pearls rest on my face as I wipe them
along with a small tear, I just shed.
For, last year, on this day you went to your grave, dear brother,
and, now you lie here, resting like a tired man who is home.

Khushboo Bhatnagar

Her name is Khushboo.She has been writing for 4 years. She is a Software Developer by profession. She loves to write stories,poems in english and hindi.She comes from Kurukshetra.

25. When I met him

It was the first time when I met him unexpectedly in the computer lab. we sit

together. We start talking and become good friends. Time passes now we start

liking each other company. Maybe we both had feeling for each other. I start

trusting him blindly. I start making soft corner for him deep inside my heart. You

came just when I wasn't looking for serious and lovely. I thought we were the

good friends but one question destroying me.

Am I falling for him?? May be yes!! May be no!! Maybe I like him or Maybe I

love him! Lost in the thoughts, my heart finally decided. I'm falling for him. I

love him. Telling him that he is my crush and then waiting for his answer is the

most difficult job. Finally, the day came. He confessed. He loves me too. And

this is how this love story begins.

We were living the bestest time. Falling for each other, expressing what is going on in mind, what is happening in day, and how much we are missing each other

in nights when nobody is around is the routine of our lives. But suddenly there is

a twist. I called him called him continuously for three days..five days..nie

days..and what all I got is "The number you are trying to reach no longer exists."

He isn't coming to college, not in contact of even his best friends, not available

at home, Parents don't know anything about him, Police is investing. It's been

two months. we are not in touch. I don't know where he is, how he is! Everyone

is tensed. I'm suffering from pain, missing him every second, Spending sleepless

nights. Hoping that he will come one day, will solve all the mysteries. Take me

out from the depression that I'm going through. I'm stuck. I myself don't know

if it is end of parts of my love story, or it will continue someday.

26. It's 4:00A.M.

I should sleep. Why the hell i am awake at this hour..! Why??

Trying to imagine..!! Trying to sleep..!! Trying to motivate myself..!! The several thoughts running on mind at this time.

What i did wrong? Why did the things mess up?

I think i should move on over my problems. I think i should promise myself that i never have to feel like i can't live without someone because if that's the case i'll never move on.

When i think about all the memories i had with the people whom i love the most and care the most, which are my priorities, I cry a little.

But,

They aren't sad and angry tears, they are happy tears because the people who leaves me with whosoever reason didn't hurt me so much. Rather than they taught me..!!

They taught me how to love situations and someone endlessly. But they also taught me how to stop loving someone and stop caring them.

And that's bad for them..!

I know what my problem is..!!

I don't realize how much pain they are causing me because they pretend to care me.

I do so much for them and thet doesn't give back to the same energy i have and i give in. How can i just forget everything??
So from now i don't care anyone. The people really wants to be with me are surely welcome. But those who don't please leave me...
DON'T make the friendship Toxic.
So from now,
I am changed..!
I no longer have patience for certain things, not because i have become arrogant,
But,
Simply because i reached at a point where i do not want waste time with what dissapoints or hurts me..!!
MAY BE THIS IS WHAT NEEDED TO HAPPEN..!!

Kunal Mehta

His name is Kunal. He has started writing 5 years back.

He is a businessman by profession. He comes from Kurukshetra - The Land of Mahabharta.

He likes to write mostly about love , heartbreaks but thats not all . We are introducing him in our publication.

27. Someday Someplace Sometime...

Someday someplace sometime a moment will come..
where we will be holding hands and walking together...
A few words, lots of emotions.. and a chilly air..
Those dawns and dusks of beautiful winter..
Behind those fog, a love will blossom..
Hugs and kisses will be new normal..
Bonfire and lovely music is still a dream..
Where the stories will be recited to our kid..
Someday.. Someplace.. Sometime....

28. An Unposted Letter

You are still so special..that i cant even forget a single thing about you...

Its been 2.5 years almost.. and still i am lost in your beauty.. wandering in your eyes...

Yups eyes... that those photographs always shown me.. at the time, i need you the most..

But someone was busy living the beautiful moments, caring, loving... Forgetting everything and smiling and here i am lost...

Lost in the thoughts that remind me of you.. lost in the moments i once lived with you.. lost in the dreams i had seen for you...

lost.. lost.. lost..... somewhere..beyond..

But still with that smile of yours.. i fell again.. How stupid i am ... Or soft hearted may be... Who still enjoy your cuteness and lame...

Yeaah that smile can do a lot ... a lot of damage...

Dont think of me ever.. if you read it somewhere one day...

I still have blessing to live... Happily.. may be.. or to live only..

Still confused with out your opinion... I should better be..stop..

Else it will be too much... Too much for us...

Oh sorry... Sorry.. Too much for me...

(And thats where two more papers were tore off..)